DUPPY
TALK

GERALD HAUSMAN

DUPPY TALK

West Indian Tales
of Mystery and Magic

Irie Books
Pine Island, Florida

Pine Island, Florida

ISBN 0-9709112-0-3

For information, address Irie Books, 12699 Cristi Way,
Bokeelia, Florida 33922 USA
Printed in Canada.

OTHER JAMAICAN BOOKS
BY GERALD HAUSMAN

Three Little Birds
(adapted with Cedella Marley
illustrated by Mariah Fox)

The Boy From Nine Miles:
The Early Life of Bob Marley
(with Cedella Marley
illustrated by Mariah Fox)

The Jacob Ladder
(with Uton Hinds)

56 Thoughts From 56 Hope Road:
The Sayings and Psalms of Bob Marley
(edited with Cedella Marley)

See the complete list at www.geraldhausman.com

ACKNOWLEDGMENTS

Much appreciation is given to Zora Neale Hurston whose *Tell My Horse* originally prompted me to visit the island of Jamaica:

> The very best place to be in all the world is St. Mary's parish, Jamaica. And the best spot in St. Mary's is Port Maria, though all of St. Mary's is fine. Old Maker put himself to a lot of trouble to make that part of the island of Jamaica, for everything there is perfect.

In the mid-eighties, I discovered as she had some forty-eight years earlier, that St. Mary was, indeed, a parish of incomparable beauty. My wife, Lorry, and I started a summer school there, just outside of Port Maria. The program, now in its ninth year, owes much to Blue Harbour on the north coast which has been our second home. And it was there, at Blue Harbour and in the village, that the tales of *Duppy Talk* grew like a night-blooming vine, whose tendrils have crept all the way into this book.

—Gerald Hausman

These stories are dedicated to the people of Castle Gordon, Port Maria, Parish of St. Mary, Jamaica, West Indies. For it was through them that I learned that proverbs are the children of experience, and stories are the parents of wisdom.

CONTENTS

INTRODUCTION

The legends in *Duppy Talk*—tales of magic power and mystic people—come from the great act of remembering.

Long ago storytellers were historians, the caretakers of memory. However, they were also much more than this. They were the workers of magic, the mystic keepers of the sacred word.

And it was through them that the people of Africa, who were brought to the Caribbean as slaves, were joined to their roots. The tribal storytellers kept the ancient gods and ghosts alive by telling stories about them.

The stories of West Indian life in this book are stories of ghost magic. They are tales that speak of the supernatural. The use of *obeah*, or black magic, was, and still is, widespread in the Caribbean. But it is not, as popularly believed, a force of evil as much as it is a ritual use of power. The obeah man, or witch doctor, became prevalent during colonial times. It was he who—by casting spells—protected his brothers and sisters from the tyranny of the slave masters. Commonly, in the old days, it was mainly men who practiced obeah. However, now women seem to be doing it as much as men.

Today, obeah men still create strange happenings—events which many of us may find hard to believe. They can cast a simple spell, concoct a love potion, call forth a ghost or *duppy*.

The word duppy comes from the African word, *dupe* or *dube*, which means spirit of the dead. Duppies are restless souls who are believed to haunt the living. Obeah men, often called upon to catch these shadows of the dead, were once called "shadow catchers."

Here are a few ways that obeah men use to catch duppies.

One way is to draw a figure eight in the earth.

Duppies, it is said, cannot count past three. Therefore, the presence of an eight drawn in the dirt stops them in their tracks. They cannot figure it out the sinuous loops as tricky as a snake.

Another way to stop a duppy is to put a *leaf of life* plant in a glass of sacred spring water. In Jamaica, the Arawak Indian land of wood and water, sacred springs are thought to have great healing power. Duppies are drawn to water, but the leaf of life—a symbol of life, not death—causes them to turn around and go back the way they came.

Drumming ceremonies also guard against duppies. Drums cleanse the air of bad spirits. The fearless sound of the drum chases away evil and tells duppies they are not welcome.

In the *nine night* ceremony the deceased person is sent off to the spirit world with a blessing from his/her family. During the eight days of the ceremony, the family gathers and plays games, drinks coffee, tea, and rum, sings the old ancestral songs, plays drums and dominoes.

On the ninth night, a plate of food is placed under a large silk-cotton tree. The plate might contain a cooked plantain, East Indian bread called *roti*, peas and rice, and perhaps, a freshly rolled cigarette. Thus the deceased person, after enjoying a last supper among the living, is requested to go on his/her journey to the spirit world alone. Obeah men do not participate in the nine night ceremony because the spirit of the dead is not—at this time—considered to be evil.

Obeah men are not the only ones who wield magic in the Caribbean. The *myalist,* or bush doctor, is an African version of a pharmacist. The Jamaican word, *myal,* comes from the African word, *maye,* or sorcerer.

Myal men and myal women are those who have a special knowledge of herbs and plants. They know all about mystical cures. The plants they use were once called "food of the gods" because it was thought that, long ago, the gods dined upon them. Today bush medicines are used to heal sickness in the Caribbean, as well as many other parts of the world. The people who administer them are no longer called myalists, they are called bush doctors.

The tales in *Duppy Talk* are based upon ancient legends. In each one we can see the roots that bind the Africa of old to the Caribbean of today. Not one of the stories told here is "made up." All have come from storytellers who live on the north coast of Jamaica.

Jamaican storytellers are some of the best in the Caribbean, perhaps among the best in the world. When a Jamaican tells a tale, it is acted out as well as told. Thus the spoken word is dramatized in a theatrical manner and the story takes on a life of its own.

I have been collecting West Indian folktales in the Caribbean for nearly thirty years, and I owe a debt of gratitude to the people who told me these stories. This debt is partially paid by *The Storyteller Speaks* sections at the end of each story. Therein the reader may experience a little more of the spoken voice of the island and some of the haunted history—the light and shadow—of the bright, dark Caribbean.

ANGELS
OF DARKNESS

SEEING IS DIFFERENT FROM BEING TOLD.
~ Proverb

Tall T, the bus driver, raised his head from the front
seat of his minibus, the Irie One, and looked out into
the thick Jamaican fog. He had fallen asleep by the
side of the road after his midnight run from Montego
Bay to Castle Gordon. Now, staring into the creepers
of fog, he rubbed his eyes, thinking he was dreaming.

Surely, what he saw was not real. It couldn't possibly be real. Or could it?

He turned on his headlights. The two bright beams bore into the foggy dark, lighting up the silhouetted figures of two barefoot little girls, both wearing high-collared, ruffled-sleeved white nightdresses.

"What are you doing out here at this time of night?" he called through the open window of the Irie One.

Neither one of them said a word. They stood haloed in the wisps of fog that faded them, their hair neatly done up in cornrows.

"Where do you live?" Tall T asked, amazed.

One of the girls raised her hand, gesturing toward the hills above Castle Gordon.

"Up there," Tall T questioned, "by Tank Lane?"

The girls nodded, slowly.

Then they came around the side of the minibus. They were holding hands, as if on their way to church. *What strange girls,* Tall T thought, *so stiff and stern they seem like little adults.*

"Well, get in," he said uneasily, "and I'll take you home. Who do you live up there with—your mommy or your auntie?"

Immediately, the two white-clothed figures climbed

up through the open door and slid onto the front seat. Neither one of them answered him.

"Are you girls new around here?" he asked.

They stared down the night highway, their eyes huge and dark and empty.

"What, in heaven's name, are you doing in your nightclothes? And why are you wandering around in the middle of the night?"

The two girls, sitting side by side, looked dreamily out into the foggy night. Lips pursed, they said not a word; and when Tall T, shaking his head, listened for the sound of their breathing, he heard nothing.

Then he started up the Irie One. The engine blatted, went nay-nay-nay, backfired once, loudly. He shut it off.

The girls sat in silence. Snakelike, the fog coiled across the road. Waiting a moment, he switched on the ignition again. "Please start," he whispered, as the reluctant engine continued naying. He cut it off again.

The girls did not move. They sat together like perfect little statues. Tall T noticed that their round heads were identical. Twins, he thought.

Again, he turned the switch. This time, though feebly, the engine caught, the Irie One started up.

"Got to get a new starter or we won't be going

anywhere, anymore." Releasing the parking brake, he turned out upon the road. The headlights poked dimly through the coarse streamers of flannel fog.

"Can't see nothin'," he mumbled to himself, wiping the ghosted windshield with an old rag.

The girls sat close, holding hands. They looked straight ahead, their mouths tight and the pupils of their eyes like black rainpools.

"I've seen some pretty crazy things in the middle of the night," Tall T said, trying to make conversation. "Once a donkey ran across the road, dragging a small man by the ankle. The poor fellow was on his back, waving his arms like a bug and the donkey was going along as if he were pulling a cart in a parade." This image never failed to make people laugh. It was a standby, and it always got at least a smile, but not tonight. The two girls, eyes trained on the fog road, said nothing.

"Well, that really wasn't so strange," he went on. "But there was another time—"

He glanced at the two silent passengers. They remained glued to the seat, eyes riveted ahead.

"As I was saying, there was the time I saw a Bengal tiger, like the kind you see in the movies—"

A quick look at the girls, whose faces registered no

surprise, told him he was talking to himself.

"—it jumped across the bridge over by Duncans. That tiger was real, you know. It had escaped from the circus."

Tall T's voice sounded strange, as if he were speaking inside an empty tunnel. The girls gazed raptly into the watery grayness. Their narrow shoulders appeared pinned together, and their stone-shaped heads bobbed only when the Irie One went over a bump. Tall T noticed that their eyes, which held the steady rhythm of the road, were as attentive as a goat's, but equally blank.

As the old bus rolled along through the thick bunting of fog, banana leaves by the roadside flapped against its fenders. The night, despite the chill, was full of the running sound of whistling toads and the glitter of potholes brimming with rainwater.

"That tiger that I was telling you about—"

Tall T, talking to himself, was beginning to admit his nervousness. Somehow, if possible, he wanted to wake them up and make them listen to him. After all, he was giving them a free ride in the ragged hours of the dewy night, a time when sensible drivers were home asleep in their own beds, not hunting through the fog, telling aimless tales of runaway tigers.

However, no matter what he said, the girls made no comment, nor movement. They had their hands joined, their shoulders stuck together, and they stared . . . and stared. And the road lapped at the wheels of the gracious old bus and swished with rivery noises when they came down the hill by Silver Sands.

Finally, Tall T made the hard right turn up toward Tank Lane. He downshifted into first gear, and the engine moaned like a brass band fading on a bad note. The valves fluttered, making the shush of maracas. Then the gear got hold of itself, and the Irie One labored up the steep road with renewed dignity.

The girls eased toward him with the tilting of the bus, their frozen postures thrown slightly off-balance. Good, he thought, at least they move once in a while.

The gears grated, the engine moaned low, as he made the slow ascent up the steep back road, which soon turned narrow and gave way to hard-packed dirt.

"My brother Tall-y lives in that house there," Tall T pointed out proudly. "He's six inches taller than I am, which makes him the tallest man in St. Mary. He drives a bus just like I do, that slick-looking red one with the funny bulge on the roof. You must've seen it, everybody has."

The girls rocked a little as the broken springs of

the Irie One took the jolts of the bumpy lane that was now turning into an old weedy cow path. "Nothing up here, girls. No houses, as I recall." He drove along very slowly now, barely creeping.

Then, for a moment, he wondered what he was doing. Had they actually said they were going up here, or had he just imagined it?

Tall T downshifted. The gears ground like glass. The Irie One was taking a beating—and for what?

"Mind if I let you out here?" he asked, half-joking, half-serious. The silence was really beginning to unnerve him.

The girls turned toward Tall T, their eyes large with alarm.

He felt a tickle along his spine. Shivering, he jerked up the collar of his coat and lowered his chin.

"You girls cold?"

They eyed him with concern, but their lips did not move; nor did they make any effort to speak.

Those eyes, he thought, would wake the dead.

They continued to press him with their twin faces of worry. And the whites of their eyes seemed to give off a bluey glow in the darkness of the bus.

"Don't worry," he comforted, "I wasn't going to pitch you out, that was just a little joke."

Then, in front of the bus, Tall T saw a tucked-away

house leaning precariously out of the dreaming bush.

"Is that your house?" he asked.

The girls did not reply.

But he saw it clearly now for what it was, actually little more than a tumbledown shack, but built in the era when gingerbread and filigree and lovely wooden fretwork were the signs of the times.

"Is that your momma's house?" he asked again.

Now the dark windows of the house filled with yellow sherry light, as a kerosene lantern was lighted inside.

The bus came to a halt in front of the paint-peeled, sagging porch. Like a lot of Jamaican houses, this one had seen better days, much better days. Then an old lady appeared in the doorway, holding a smoking kerosene lamp whose light swam eerily about the old porch. She was wearing a long white nightdress in the Victorian fashion of years gone by.

Tall T opened his door and went around to let his two eager passengers out. Yes, he thought, by their excited eyes, this had to be their home, and if not their mom, their grandma or their auntie was now awaiting them.

"I never got your names," he said, as he helped them down to the wet clumped Bermuda grass.

The moment their bare feet touched the ground, they shot away toward the porch, and the old lady—

lantern and all—enfolded them in her arms. Then the three of them went inside the decrepit house, and the last thing Tall T saw was the old lady's nightdress as it sucked itself into the door. The blurry gold light leaped around the windows of the fallen-down house, and then it, too, was extinguished, and the night of fogs and toads took over once again.

"If that don't beat the pants off runaway tigers . . ." Tall T grumbled, getting back into the Irie One. "Not one of them thanked me."

After turning around, he drove down the mountain under the dripping groves of flowering trees. The tires crunched on the thin, dry pods of the poincianas. Presently, he came to his brother Tall-y's house.

There was an electric light on inside. Tall-y must be getting up to go to work, he thought. Tall T ground the Irie One to a halt, felt the broken springs complain, as usual, and then he turned off the engine.

Looking toward the hilltop, there was a rose-colored glimmer where the old lady's house had been. But Tall T knew this was the coming of the dawn.

Tall-y was already dressed, stooping around in his tiny kitchen, making himself a pot of tea. Tall T gladly accepted some, and his brother poured a syrupy stream of condensed milk into the cup, sweetening it to perfection.

Then Tall-y sat down, and the two brothers looked at each other for the first time and began to laugh very softly. This was how they always started their conversations. Tall-y would open his mouth, start to say something, and the two of them would laugh at the same time.

"What do you know," Tall T said, "all these years, you've been living on this hill, and I never knew you had a neighbor up top."

Tall-y's wide brow furrowed. He had a deep, rough, gravelly voice that sounded like the sea chafing against the rocks.

"No neighbor up top," he rumbled hoarsely, sipping the hot tea, "not for a long, long time, anyways."

Tall T said, "I just took two little girls home to their granny. The last run of the night—for no fare. They live way up on top of Tank Lane."

"An old granny, you say?" Tall-y's low voice crept up an octave. "There hasn't been an old granny on that hill since before you and I were babies. What are you talking about?"

"I am talking," Tall T said tiredly, "about two little girls. They were out on the road, looking for a ride to their grandmother's house. I picked them—no, the other way around—they picked me up. Well, anyway,

I delivered them to their door—two little girls in old-fashioned white nightdresses."

He took a swallow of the sweet, sugary tea, and smiled weakly at Tall-y who was now looking at him with sharpened eyes.

"Brother," Tall-y breathed loudly, "you've been upon the road for too many hours."

Tall T put his face into his hands, trying to rub away the fatigue with his fingers. The hot day, the long night, the close fog, the need for sleep—all these had suddenly caught up with him. And the last thing he wanted was an argument with Tall-y.

Outside the dawn was splashing the hills red. "Let's go outside, get a breath of air," Tall T said.

Tall-y, stooping low to pass through the front door, followed his brother into the morning light. They drank the rest of their tea under the limbs of a flame heart tree. The black bark was burning with tiny rubies of dew.

Tall T felt clean in the coming light. "First day of creation," he mused. Then, handing Tall-y his teacup, he opened the door of the Irie One. Whispering the words, "Thanks and praises," his prayer of the morning, he turned the key. The reluctant engine, always slow to catch, immediately began to purr.

Tall-y came around slowly, put his big, friendly

face in the open window. He was smiling. "Listen, brother," he said, "You ought to know something. There was an old granny burned up her house back before you were born. She caught herself on fire, so they say. There's nothing left of her place on the hill but a couple rusty nails."

Tall T shook his head. "There were two little girls," he said, "two little . . . " his voice trailed off.

"Those were little angels, if you ask me," Tall-y replied.

"Angels . . . not . . . duppies?"

"That's right. Duppies don't try to save any old granny," Tall-y said, "that's angel business. Besides," he laughed, "if it was two little duppies, your old Irie One wouldn't have turned over so quick. Sounds like she got a good charming herself."

Tall T began to laugh. Tall-y brother was right. The Irie One had started with one turn of the key, and that hadn't happened since the day he bought her.

And, as Tall T looked up the mountain, the dawn sun seemed to have set the poincianas on fire. The two brothers looked at each other and laughed. The rising sun had washed away the darkness and chased away the gray snakes of fog. The new day was crisp and fresh.

"I guess those two little girls were angels after all,"

Tall T told his brother Tall-y. And they grinned as only brothers can grin, their smile coming from the same heart, which is the beginning of the world. And from that time on, the Irie One, which, in Jamaican, means good tidings, has always started on the first try.

And always will, Tall T says.

THE STORYTELLER SPEAKS

Tall T is the shortest of four brothers. The tallest brother is, of course, Tall-y. The next tallest is Tony Skank, and the next after him is Winston, also known as Bup. Tall T is well over six foot in height. Tall-y is seven foot.

Now, the only thing taller than Tall-y is his laugh. He has a very tall laugh. I once made a recording of Tall-y laughing and took it home to play for some of my friends who thought it was the sea splashing on the rocks.

If Tall T, or any of his brothers, were hanging around telling stories, sooner or later the mood might shift to duppies who travel along the roadside. In Jamaica they say that duppies do not like headlights or cars moving about, so you don't see them that often on the brightly lit highway, but rather on the dark roadside night. There is the old Indian woman wearing a sari, or scarf, around her whole body, who begs bread from all who stop. Once you give her something, she vanishes. And there is the rolling calf that falls downhill in a terrible clatter of chains, blowing fire from its mouth and nose. This story with its chains and flames comes from the slave legends of long ago.

It is said, today, that if you want to see the rolling calf, or rollen calf, as they say in patois (island talk), you must wait for independence day, which comes on the first Monday of August. The legend states that at this time, the celebration of the end of slavery in Jamaica (1834), many "plantation duppies" appear at night. These include the rolling calf whose chains are symbols of slavery.

Roadside tales of duppies are common in Jamaica, especially stories of duppies meeting on crossroads. Wherever there is a drawn X or a cross on the road, duppies have to stop because they do not know what to make of it. Since roads make natural Xs and crosses, they are often places where duppies stand confused.

They say, in Jamaica, that angels are ruled by myal

men or myal women. These are the workers of white, or good, magic.

Duppies, as we already know, are ruled by obeah men or obeah women. The story of the two little angels told here was related to me by Tall T after he had visited a myal woman in Montego Bay. There are, he said, good spirits and bad. Surely, the little girls were good spirits, angels who brought him safely home to Tank Lane.

If you ever find yourself on the double bend between Castle Gordon and Port Maria late at night, you should pay special attention to the road. In addition to the Indian woman in the sari, the rolling calf, the two little girls in their white nightdresses, you might also see the old penner. This is the farmer who wears high leather boots and who carries a long whip and drives a herd of ghost cattle home to their pen. Be careful, you could drive right through them—with no harm to anyone—yet the old penner will stand in the road, after you have passed; he'll crack his whip and shout, "Rude, rude, rude!"

DUKE
OF LUCK

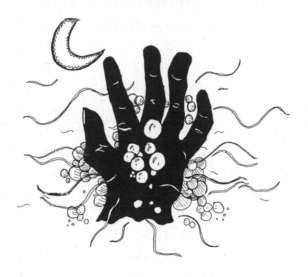

WHEN ONE DOOR IS CLOSED, ANOTHER IS OPENED.
~ Proverb

"Things have gone from bad to worse," Tony muttered to himself. He had less than five dollars in his pocket, hardly enough for cocoa bread and a cup of fish tea. First, he'd lost his job; then, his wife had left him. Now, he felt so out of luck, he was sure that if a coconut were to fall out of a tree, he would be walking right under it and would get it on the head.

Mumbling about his bad luck, he headed toward Fisherman's Beach. There, at least, he might smell the food cooking. Perhaps someone who knew him would lend him some money. Then, after a small meal, he might refresh himself with a nice swim in the sea.

His palm itched, which was a good sign. That meant some luck. Then, riding in a minibus, he heard a woman sneeze. That was the best sign of all; a woman sneezing meant riches were coming his way.

At Fisherman's Beach, Tony's old friend Chef Joe granted him a lunch on credit. He sat in the shade of a banana leaf and stared at the sea. The cocoa bread was hot, the fresh butter melting in the middle. The fish tea, served in a gourd, was tasty and it filled his empty belly.

So, maybe my luck is on the mend, Tony thought. The signs seem so, anyway. Now that I have food in my stomach, maybe I can think this thing through.

Staring into the blue bay, he thought about the people in the world who never have to worry about money. And that was where his nagging doubts began once again.

He stared at the tourists splashing in the surf and wished he were one of them. "What have they done to deserve such uncommon luck?" he wondered. But before he could ponder the answer—if there was one—a large brown face appeared before him.

It was his cousin Earl, the one they called "Lucky Duke."

"What's up, Duke?" Tony smiled with false confidence, hiding his desolation.

"Nothing much," Duke answered, biting his lower lip. Then he sat down heavily, and scooping a handful of sand into his palm, sprinkled it through his fingers.

"Would that it were gold," he coughed. Then he added with a pained smile, "Perhaps it is, who can know?"

"You all right, man?" Tony asked, concerned.

Duke smiled weakly. Then, without looking up, he rolled upon his right side, holding his chest.

Tony saw blood on Duke's jacket.

He started to open it, but Duke pulled it tight.

"I'm dying," Duke said through clenched teeth. "No use trying to kid you . . . or myself."

"—What happened?"

"No time to talk . . . cousin," Duke choked, his face knotted. Then, "Someone . . . thought . . . I was . . . someone else," he stammered.

"What can I do?" Tony asked.

Duke tried to say something. His eyes worked to form the words that his mouth was unable to shape.

"Don't talk," Tony suggested. "Just lie still."

Duke said, "My poor pickney . . . Pansy."

His eyes filled with tears.

Tony cradled Duke's head. "Whatever I have, she will have," he said. "Don't worry about Pansy."

Duke smiled. "I knew I could count on you."

Then Duke's body arched, once, and grew still.

Tony stared in disbelief.

Duke was dead.

For the rest of that afternoon Tony sat in a spell of silence. His cousin, Lucky Duke, lay next to him, dead. Yet Duke looked like a man on holiday, enjoying a snooze by the sea. He looked anything but dead.

How could this have happened? Tony wondered.

Duke was the lucky one—lucky in love and in work, lucky in life. Tony remembered the time when they were beachcombing together. Tony found some rusted aerosol cans, a toothbrush covered with tar, a barnacle-encrusted license plate. Duke discovered a worthless coconut, but when he cracked it open, there was a roll of hundred dollar bills inside. And the money was not even wet. That was the kind of luck Duke had.

Lucky Duke.

He was also the first person in the family to pass the Common Entrance Exam and thus be admitted into high school. This was very difficult to do; and Duke had done it without any tutoring. He was blessed, all right.

However, Duke's great good luck had finally run out. For he was dead.

Then Tony's thinking changed. Maybe, he thought, it is something else. Perhaps it is as our grandmother used to say: "God loves them the most, the ones who are taken first."

Yes, he reasoned. That is the best way to look at death.

How it had happened didn't matter much to Tony. What mattered was that he must now provide for Pansy, Duke's daughter. He had promised to do so, but with the kind of rotten luck that he'd been having, he wondered how he was going to go about it.

At dusk the day's freshness left the air, and the nighttime cool, the wind they call the "Undertaker's Breeze," came up from the headland and combed the sea grape leaves along the beachfront. Tony had no idea how long he had been there. Time was measurable in shadows, but he did not see them. They stole across the sand, turning the gold grains to lusterless gray.

Finally, Tony got to his feet. Brushing sand off his bare legs, he reminded himself that he had come to the beach to eat and have a swim.

That was—how many hours ago?

Seven, eight?

He'd totally lost track of time.

He looked at the sky. It was night now. The moon was out, whitening the ruffled palms. The waves made crisp lace upon the beach. The air was cool. The silver sea inviting.

Tony took off his short-sleeved shirt and stepped into the water. A little wave tickled his ankles.

Then he felt a gentle, but firm, push between his shoulders. Looking around, he checked to see if anyone was there. The beach was deserted. The moonlit air whispered among the sea grapes. Duke appeared to be sleeping where Tony had left him. The shadow of a Panama palm made a frilly blanket that, strangely enough, covered all but his head.

Tony felt it again. The push.

The nudge between his shoulders.

"Who's there?"

He felt foolish saying the words out loud. No one was there.

He was alone.

Tony glanced into the pretty moon sparks of Fisherman's Beach. Then, for no reason, he knelt and scooped up a handful of them. "Would that these dancing bits of moon were precious gems," Tony said.

And his hand closed on something firm.

His fingers came together, closing on something real . . . *Is this happening? Or am I completely losing my mind?*

He ran back to the beach, grabbed his canvas beach bag, and returned to the foaming shore.

Then, once more, he knelt in the lilting sea.

They were everywhere. And as fast as he could scoop them up, his hands were filled with gleaming, gloaming pebbly magic. His fingers closed, and they bubbled through the cracks. Time after time, he emptied his dripping fists into the beach bag, and then, returning to harvest more, he plunged back into the bounty.

When the bag was full, Tony went back one more time. Burying his hands in the froth, he stared at the mountain of moonlit pearls that he'd been gathering for over an hour.

His heart bumped in his chest. There were enough pearls here to last several lifetimes, and yet, if he wanted them, his hands could reach out and take more—and more.

However, the realization struck him, then, that he could do no such thing.

For the hands in the salty moon water were not his— they belonged to someone else.

Where was the scar he had gotten on that piece

of coral when he was eight?

Where was the missing knuckle on his pinkie, the one cut off on the bicycle chain when he was eleven?

Where, he wanted to know, were his own meager fingers?

Slowly, it came to him that the hands he beheld in the shimmering water, the hands feasting on pearls, were not his own. Short and stubby, these were the hands of another man. He recognized them, though. They belonged to Lucky Duke. Quickly, he looked toward the place where Duke was lying. He was still there. The shadow blanket of palm frond covered all of him now.

Then, in the time that it takes to think such a thing, the odd, square-shaped fingers turned back into his own long, slender ones.

Tony stood up, his heart pounding.

Were the pearls real?

Or were they, too, some art or act of other-worldly magic?

He went to the canvas bag and looked inside. It was engorged with creamy blue pearls, the size of marbles.

Hefting the bag upon his shoulder, Tony walked back to where he'd taken off his shirt and shoes. Duke looked peaceful, his face so far from care, so close to heaven.

And Tony knew that wherever Duke was, luck was with him. For look how much of it he had shared already.

THE STORYTELLER SPEAKS

We were singing songs in the moonlight when Tony reminded us that our drums were thirsty. "You cannot play a drum without giving it a little drink, now and then," he said. Then he poured some dark rum on the goatskin head, rubbing the rum around the drum's rim and across the surface of the taut skin.

The next notes I played were suddenly lively and fresh. "That is a happy drum sound," Tony said, smiling. It was then that I saw him pour a half cup of dark rum onto the earth.

"Is the earth thirsty, too?" I asked.

"Yes," he said, "she gets thirsty, too. However, this one is for Duke."

"Your cousin, the one who was accidentally shot in Ocho Rios?"

He nodded, corking the rum bottle.

"Duke, my lucky, lucky cousin."

"I would like to know more about him."

"Well," Tony smiled, "He was a man who if you passed him on the street, you wouldn't notice him. You would have had to know him. He was the luckiest man alive."

"Why do you think so?"

"Because he knew what it meant to be alive and to share that knowledge. He was always sharing what he had, what he knew. Every moment was a special moment when you were with him. He just seemed to glory in life—to take nothing for granted. So, therefore, all who knew him were blessed. When I touch the earth now, I touch Duke's heart, for that is where it will always reside."

Duke's luck in the story again refers to the ancient legend of the myal men, who were also known as angel men. Their luck, so-called, was not chance or merely good fortune. It was the faith that all good things come from the Great Maker, God. Myal men were those who could "pull out the bad and put in the good." Therefore, they were lucky people, indeed, and could pass this exceptional gift on to others. Duke proved his own power and grace by passing his luck on to Tony and his daughter, Pansy, after he died.

LAUGHTER OF MERMAIDS

THE MIND DOESN'T SEE WHAT
THE HEART CAN'T LEAP.
~ Proverb

They were standing under the blue shadow of an African tulip tree—the Jamaican bush doctor, Mackie McDonnough, and his young apprentice, Alec Thompson.

"Do you know the name of this tree?" Mackie questioned.

"Flame of the forest," Alec answered quickly.

The roadbed where they stood was littered with giant, red torchlike blossoms that seemed to smoulder on the summer tar.

Mackie smiled with approval, but his smile soon faded.

"And what is that tree over there?" he asked sharply.

"Guango."

"—Which comes from . . . ?"

"Africa."

"Hah!" Mackie laughed. "Your father will be happy to hear that these lessons he arranged were not in vain. Now, if you can tell me one more thing . . ."

Mackie looked curiously at his pupil.

"Yes?"

"How come you sweat so much?"

Alec, whose clothes were already soaked, smiled uncertainly. There was no escaping the weather in Jamaica—especially in the summer. The thick air was like a hot net, and the temperature was ninety degrees in the shade. However, Mackie, the miraculous bush doctor, was cool as talc, dry as dust.

His face—and how Alec marveled at its curves and color—was teak. Like a deeply shadowed African mask, his expressions were hidden. The furrows on either side of his nose ran riverlike down his face, disappearing near his chin, while his almond-shaped eyes danced with darkness.

Mackie was a man of mystery, a magical being who seemed to swim in and out of the shadows. His walk was an open invitation to move freely with the natural rhythm of nature. But Alec, who tried in vain to imitate it, always ended up feeling foolish.

Often Alec compared Mackie to his own father, who was a very stuffy sort of man. He, too, was a bush doctor, in a way. Actually, he was a Canadian pharmacologist.

Tall and reedy looking, Alec's father towered over most Jamaicans, including Mackie. But he was shy and edgy, and fearful of people. He talked rapidly, sometimes stuttering, frequently interrupting. Alec loved his father, but he resented him, too. He wished his father were . . . more natural, more relaxed, like Mackie.

Mackie didn't speak, as Alec's father did, out of nervousness, or to break an uncomfortable silence. For Mackie, silence and shadow were the medium in which he lived. He liked darkness, and he liked quiet. Small of stature, he was large of manner, so that his true size usually went unnoticed.

The only trouble with Mackie was that Alec always felt like such a kid around him. His father might make him nervous, but Mackie made him feel inferior. It had something to do with Mackie being black and Alec feeling a little too white. Not that he wanted to change the color of his skin, but, at the same time, he wished it were not so noticeable that he was a pasty little white boy.

Mackie was teaching Alec Jamaican patois. Learning the language of the island made Alec feel more a part of it. But when he was speaking patois, Mackie's words flew like sparks. His phrases depended on his moods. When he was irritated, he spoke hard, pinging patois. When he was pleased, however, he spoke gentle patois, the kind that made Alec feel like he, too, was an islander.

They were halfway down Firefly hill, above Castle Gordon, when Mackie pointed at a creeper vine.

"Yuh know dis ting?" he sang out, his voice ringing to the pitch of patois.

Alec recognized the leaf of a *cerasee* plant, from which Mackie frequently brewed a special herbal tea. As far as Alec was concerned, cerasee was the nastiest, bitterest tea he'd ever tasted. However, Mackie insisted that it was great for the liver: a cleanser, a tonic.

He'd tried some, as part of the course, and sure enough, just as Mackie said, it cleared his complexion. Mackie was always right.

"Cerasee," Alec said confidently.

"Good fe eat?" Mackie asked.

Alec knew a trick question when he heard one.

"It's a medicine, you've got to drink it."

Mackie smiled. Then, stripping off an orange pod from the green vine, Mackie popped it open. Inside were some small, grayish seeds. He put a few into his mouth, offering Alec the rest.

Alec, remembering how bitter cerasee tea was, put the seeds on his tongue expecting to spit them out. Sucking on them, he discovered they had no taste.

"Go ahead, bite dem," Mackie insisted.

Grimacing, Alec started to chew them.

"Hey, these taste like sunflower seeds!" Alec said, surprised.

Mackie chuckled, "Sometime coffee, sometime tea."

"What does that mean?" Alec asked, putting more cerasee seeds in his mouth.

"Different ting fe different ting."

"Oh, I get it. In English you say, 'sometimes water, sometimes wine.' "

Mackie nodded. "Now, Alec, you can wash yuh face wid dis?"

"—Can . . . what?"

Playfully, Mackie waved the vine of cerasee in Alec's face, tickling his chin with the feathery leaves.

"Any ting wrong wid de skin, cerasee cure. Yuh can wash wid dis, mon."

Alec remembered. He'd heard about cerasee baths on another walk in the bush.

Mackie stooped down and fetched something from the earth. Opening his palm, he revealed a handful of seeds. Each one had the red eye of a tropical bird.

"Yuh know dis ting?"

"John Crow bead," Alec grinned.

"You know your lessons well," Mackie confirmed.

"Mackie?"

"Yah, mon."

"You think we could take some time off today?"

Mackie looked thoughtfully at Alec, sizing him up.

"Your father's so particular about these lessons," he reminded him. "He believes that when you move here permanently, this learning will come in handy."

"That's if I decide to be like him."

Mackie showed the trace of a wry smile.

"What do you dream to do, Alec?"

"I want to be a bush doctor, like you—"

Mackie gave a sudden, cackling "Hah!" Then, chuckling, he said, "You make more money as an obeah man."

"There's one other thing I dream to do."

"And what is that?"

"I would like you to teach me something," Alec sighed, "something not in any of the books on plants and stuff. Some special kind of medicine . . . "

"What about a medicine for the mind?" Mackie asked mysteriously.

"You mean—a drug?"

Mackie shook his head. Then he gave Alec a penetrating look as if he were seeing into him. Looking away, his eyes followed a flock of emerald pocket parrots, bickering as they flew into a grove of mango trees.

Alec felt, just then, that Mackie had gone off with those parrots. That was the way he was.

"What's a medicine for the mind—if not a drug of some kind?" Alec asked.

Mackie tossed the pretty red seeds that looked like tropical birds' eyes into the bush. "The mind is just like the heart," he answered simply, "but it wants food of a different kind."

Eyeing the upper limbs of the jungle trees, he seemed to be searching for something out of reach, something beyond the scope of the human eye.

"Weh de gourdy dem?" he said sharply.

Alec flinched at the sudden patois. He blinked, trying to narrow his vision, tighten the margin of things seen, make the things that were invisible come into focus. This was what Mackie had taught him to do. Was this the mind-medicine Mackie meant?

Mackie asked again, "Weh de gourdy dem?"

Alec looked in earnest for the hidden globes of fruit. Somewhere, above their heads, in that secret sea of leafy green, Mackie had seen some golden gourds.

But where were they?

Alec scanned the upper levels of leaves, saw nothing familiar. Everything blended in, looked the same. He knew what they looked like, if he could just see them.

Then he saw a flash of yellow, a globe shape, peeking out of the greenery.

"Up there," Alec pointed. "Dere," he added for emphasis, smiling triumphantly.

Mackie scowled, his face turning into an Ashanti mask made of black mahogany.

"—They're there, I can see them!" Alec proclaimed.

"Breadfruit!" Mackie roared, laughing until his sides shook.

Then he said "Hah!" and shook his head meaningfully. After this, he shrugged and started down the steep trail to Castle Gordon, chuckling all the while.

Halfway down the mountain, he said over his shoulder, "Alec, you know as well as I do, that breadfruit's got alligator skin. Gourdy's smooth—like a baby's bottom."

He's talking English, Alec thought, it's a good sign.

When he caught up to him again, he asked, "Mackie, what is that medicine for the mind? I really want to know."

"That's for another lesson—when you are ready," Mackie replied somberly.

They walked the rest of the way down the mountain in silence. The sun climbing steadily toward noon was now bearing down. Even in the shade of the bush, Alec felt the heat wafting about him. His heart beat loudly as he walked. Sweat, running down his armpits, tickled his sides. He thought of Mackie twenty yards ahead, cool as a cucumber; his pimento walking stick tap-tapping the dirt trail as he went along.

Occasionally, as the trail came out of the bush and into an opening, Alec felt the cool breath of the sea. Now he longed to be away from the bush, to be off by himself, to be finished with his bush lessons.

All around him were the hanging vines, the prison bars of decay. He had an urge to break through the canopies of leaves, to leap free of everything. He watched Mackie flowing through the bush. He wondered if he, Alec, were denied this freedom because . . . of the color of his skin.

For it seemed to him that being white meant he couldn't blend in with the shades of color all around him.

In the silence, Alec saw his pale skin. Mackie, a few steps ahead of him, moved, actually melted into the shadows. At times, he would disappear into the darkness, emerging with a face that masked his feelings. He is like a chameleon, Alec decided. He fits in wherever he goes.

They walked on until, at the bottom of the hill, they came to a small blue spring that bubbled out of the white lime-crusted rocks.

Mackie bent down, wetting his face and neck. Then he drank some of the spring water with a cupped palm.

"Here you are," he said coaxingly. "Here is your medicine for the mind."

Mackie drank thirstily, smiling so that the shape of his face, which was usually hard, grew soft and expectant.

"This spring's been here since before Arawak time," he whispered. "The old people who live in the hills say that the water's blessed."

"By who?" Alec asked.

Mackie shrugged, looked absently around for a place to sit. He liked to crouch, a position that Alec imitated badly.

"The old people say there's a mermaid that guards the spring," Mackie said.

Alec looked into the blue water and saw that it bubbled pleasantly.

"Go ahead, drink it, mon."

Alec couldn't have explained why he hesitated. The sparkling water looked cold and good to drink. He was very thirsty, and the spring beckoned, but it also seemed forbidden. He wondered whether drinking the spring water would make him—somehow—

feel less than he already was.

"Go ahead," Mackie laughed, "it won't hurt you."

Alec dropped to his knees. In his mind, he felt that he was actually surrendering to the jungle, giving up.

He put his face into the cold water and opened his eyes.

At once he saw the mermaid staring at him.

Her head appeared larger than the rest of her body because of the swirling of her hair.

As she moved her lips, Alec heard her speak.

"What are you doing here, boy?"

"Drinking."

Her skin was the color of dark honey, and all around her head, her gold, wiry hair rose and fell like water-weeds in the secret current. He saw when she smiled that she had little gray teeth, fishlike and sharp. Around her head and hair, there fanned a school of bright minnows.

The mermaid saw him looking at the fish.

"My children," she remarked, "my babies."

He said nothing.

The children of the mermaid were whirling about her gold seaweed hair, making crescents and curves with their shiny fins.

"Tell me, boy, what do you eat?"

Alec followed the spinning gyre of fish with his eye.

"What do I eat? Why, fish, of course."

At this, she turned tail and plunged to the bottom of the spring, her children sparkling down into the deeper water with her. Alec could see them, glimmering in the blue depths of the fathomless pool.

Suddenly, the mermaid's large head came back to confront him. The children returned also, making a fiery halo around the tawny gold of her floating face.

"Boy, do you think I'm afraid of you?"

"No, I don't."

She smiled, faintly.

"I won't kill you, this time," she said petulantly. "But you must be warned. The next time, I will."

"I apologize."

"You should always say, when I ask that question, that you eat only from the salt sea. Do you understand?"

"I understand."

The babies fanned all about the mermaid in an ever expanding circle, winding a saturnine ring around her head, their silvery sides gleaming like blades.

Again, she smiled, her sharp little teeth appearing in her wide, full-lipped mouth.

"My children are *fresh*, but you eat only *salt*. Do you understand, boy, that you must say this right?"

Suddenly Alec felt the spell of the mermaid's eyes. He

was going deeper and deeper into the blue water. She was, somehow, pulling him in. His heart shuddered. He jerked his head out of the spring, gasping for air.

Mackie was there, as before, sitting calmly in the sun-lit grass of the glade. His face showed no hint of anything, but his eyes were smiling.

Alec struggled to get to his feet. His limbs felt sodden and numb, like a couple of well-soaked logs.

"Something the matter?" Mackie asked, his eyes twinkling.

"Everything's—all right," Alec said. His voice sounded like he was talking through a tube.

He was breathing very deeply, trying to make the light-headedness go away. The trees kept swimming in and out of his vision; the sky kept collapsing on him.

Mackie said nothing. He sat under the almond trees as cool and remote as ever. But his eyes were dancing. He looked, Alec thought, very content.

Alec blinked and the fuzzy-edged world went away. There was now a glow coming off things, a clear light that was almost comforting. Inside, in his belly, he felt a similar glow, a round good warmth.

He wanted to say something, but he had no idea what it was.

Mackie said, "Did you say something, Alec?"

There was a delicate tone to the way Mackie said his

name: softly, the way a father speaks to a son.

"No," Alec answered, "I didn't say anything, but . . . I wanted to."

"Then why didn't you?" It was the same soft voice.

"I guess, I didn't know what to say."

Alec saw clearly now that Mackie's face was alight with wonder. Had it always been like that?

Then, he heard Mackie laugh. It was a large laugh that came from the center of him, the laugh of a much larger man.

Alec listened. The laughter was everywhere. It came from the earth and the sky, the leaves and the seeds, the flowering almonds and the burning hibiscus. It came from the sun and the sea, and from all around, and it rippled and danced like a ring of bright fish.

Alec listened, and realized that the laughter was not coming from Mackie, but from himself.

He was laughing. He, Alec, was making an outrageously happy noise with his mouth. For perhaps the first time in his life, Alec was laughing with his heart and his head, as if the two were really connected, joined in the middle by a boy named Alec, a boy who was now enjoying himself, laughing as he had never laughed before.

He was the laugh man of the world, and he was sharing his feelings with all living things.

And the pleasure came up out of him, bubbling, and it was not coming from the lost white boy who was afraid of the bush.

It was the laughter of light itself and the laughter of clear blue bottomless water. It was these, and more. Yes, much more.

It was the laughter of mermaids.

THE STORYTELLER SPEAKS

The bush doctor, Mackie McDonnough, was born in St. Ann, the same parish where Bob Marley, Marcus Garvey, and Winston Rodney (Burning Spear) were born. Mackie knew Marley and Rodney, and he met people who had actually known the great black liberator, Marcus Garvey.

A descendant of the Ashanti people of the west coast of Africa, Mackie is hard-as-a-nut—his reserve impossible to crack, especially if you are a stranger. He is slightly less formal, though not much, once you know him.

The magic of Mackie is his ability to explain the secret lore told to him by his grandmother. Everything that he knows, he knows deeply. His silences speak of this, as well as his words. His manner of teaching might seem strict to some, but then, that is because he does not believe that knowledge comes lightly. To Mackie, knowledge is a gift. A gift that must be honored and won.

The mermaid, known to Mackie and many others in the village of Castle Gordon, is an old legend, much like the Holy Grail. Some say that by meeting the mermaid, a person gains some special sight, and is blessed. This mermaid myth may have come to Jamaica from the sailors of the British Isles. However, coastal Africa also has such lore.

The storyteller who told me of the mermaid in Castle Gordon is an old man by the name, coincidentally, of Mr. Gardner. His nickname, which is the one everybody uses, is "Swee-Swee"; and, while many have heard the mermaid story, few have actually laid eyes on her.

Mr. Gardner is the only person in Castle Gordon who actually met the mermaid. According to some, he was a little "touched" after the encounter. His description of her face is less than lovely, for to Mr.

Gardner, she must guard her children. She is, therefore, a bit scary looking. Her head, he says, is too large for her body. Her teeth are sharp, like an animal's.

Yet, when Mr. Gardner starts singing her praises, she becomes as beautiful and as enchanting as she is strange. If you answer her questions properly, he says, her beauty will befriend you. However, if you answer her wrongly, she may be said to touch you with another kind of magic. Alec, in the story, is given a taste of both worlds. The end result, though, is positive. He becomes, through this initiation, a true islander: one who knows things for what they are, which is why he laughs so hard at the end of the story. This was the medicine for the mind of which Mackie spoke.

Another version of the Mr. Gardner mermaid tale came to me from Roy McKay. It was Roy who said that anyone greedy would not be able to drink at the mermaid's well or spring. Once he took me there. The water in the spring had dried up; the mermaid was gone. But her spirit, he explained, was still there. After reciting some verses from the Bible, Roy poured a libation of white rum all around the spring. He then poured chicken's blood in the same circle, and said that we should return to the spring in three days' time. Three days later, just as he said, the water was back. It was, he said, the spirit of the mermaid that replenished the spring.

Sometime after this, I was walking to the spring, in the hope of seeing the mermaid, when I caught sight of a small cave by the sea. I looked inside and found, much to my amazement, a boy, two or three years old. He was standing at the mouth of the cave. He seemed oddly shaped for so small a child. His head was too large for his slender body. The boy spoke no English, only patois, which he sang rather than spoke.

Whenever I asked where his parents were, he pointed to the sea. I saw nothing out there but flashing blue water. So I went and got my friend Julie, who questioned the boy in patois. He paid her the compliment of saying that she looked like a mongoose. Julie laughed at this, the boy scowled, and then he shrank back into the cave.

Thinking he might be hungry, Julie and I went up to the kitchen and collected some food. When we returned, a few minutes later, the boy was gone. The cave was empty. There were some tracks leading into the sea. They looked like the tracks of a seal, for the toes were webbed. There is also a tale of sulkies, sea people who are part human and part seal, but that is for another book.

CHICK CHICK

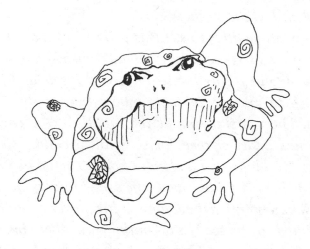

**THE WOMAN IS LIKE A SHADOW;
THE MAN IS LIKE AN ARROW.**
~ Proverb

She could hear the creature crawling on the zinc roof of the house. There was a long moment of silence. Then came the thump, telling her that the creature had moved, that it was coming after her.

Through the long night, until the crowing of the cock at dawn, the awful noises kept her awake. Then, with the first rays of the sun, they went away.

Everyone in the village of Castle Gordon knew that an obeah man had set himself against Flora, and was trying to kill her. And everyone knew that from dusk until dawn, the obeah man's evil was working to get into her house. But there was nothing anyone could do about it.

One day Flora went up to Zion Hill to pay the obeah man a visit.

"Why you set this thing upon me?" she demanded, when she was let into the obeah man's office. Flora stared at the red tile floor, polished hard and bright with Genie wax. She was not yet prepared to look into the obeah man's eyes, so she stared at the floor.

Outside in the noon sun, a long line of people waited under the palm trees. They were sitting on stones, leaning against palm trunks. There were men, women, and children—all of them waiting to see the obeah man, the sorcerer named Chick Chick. He was a man who could work miracles, arrange disasters, or create a little of each, depending on the customer's desire and urgency, and the amount of currency in hand.

Flora looked around the airless little room. It was full of ceramic statues. Hundreds, thousands of them.

Images of heroic animals, biblical saints, the Virgin Mary, comic strip characters, assorted wild beasts, and creatures of legend. In the midst of this mad gallery, Chick Chick, the obeah man, sat like a king upon a throne. His fat fingers were covered with gold rings studded with tiny diamonds. The poor people of St. Mary made him rich. He fed off them, dining on their weakness. And every day he became more powerful.

Chick Chick was secure and self-assured. He studied Flora, who refused to meet his eye. Turning away from him, she gazed at the replicas of the Virgin Mary beside which stood a row of Lassies and Rin Tin Tins. Flora looked around the room—anywhere but at Chick Chick, who smiled complacently, his round chin resting on his fat fist, glittering with diamonds.

"What is it, woman? Speak up!"

"Every night," she said, "I have an evil visitor."

Chick Chick's face brightened.

"Evil?" he questioned, eyes glinting. His bass voice rumbled in his barrel chest.

"Don't tease," she snapped. "You know what I am talking about. For it is you who sends this thing. On account . . . "

"On account—of what?" he said teasingly.

Flora glanced at the thousand statues which seemed to stare at her accusingly. Bullwinkle Moose, Daffy Duck, Smokey the Bear, and all the others. The icons were in league with Chick Chick. They were his accomplices, they worked for him.

"Ever since I couldn't pay you that money—"

"Money? What money?" He smiled graciously, showing off his gold teeth.

"A year ago, I came to you. I needed a passport to go to the United States. You put some *kananga* water on my documents, and blessed them. Then you promised I would move to the front of the line at Immigration."

"And . . . ?" He looked at her imploringly, his face full of mock compassion.

"None of that worked!" she exclaimed. "The officer passed me by. He let someone else go in, instead of me. I stayed there all day, waiting, hoping. Your magic didn't work."

"So, then you decided not to pay poor Chick Chick for his services. Am I correct?"

"I haven't any money!"

For the first time, she looked briefly into his eyes, which were milky blue. His skin was the high color of straw after it is cut and turns brown in the sun.

The change came quickly. The child eyes of Chick Chick became cold and cruel. He remained calm. She stood there, trembling. She'd willed herself to be strong, but now she was weakening. She started to wring her hands. Chick Chick bore down on her with his bass voice.

"I am warning you. Pay up—or I shall have to—"

"I'll call the police," she said weakly.

Laughing scornfully, he said, "Before they ever come to check me, an unwanted visitor will have found its way into your house."

He chuckled into his diamond-studded fist. Flora rushed out of the office, her face streaming with tears.

That night, Flora made certain that her door was bolted, her windows shuttered in place, locked from the inside. She made sure her one-room house was tight as a drum. Preparing for bed, she moved the coarse *kaya* mattress into the center of the floor.

On a night table, made from a discarded saltfish box, she placed her holy candle. The slender flame swam clearly in the darkness, as if seeking to rise higher.

Flora began to recite her favorite psalms. She said them from start to finish. Then she repeated them over again. The more psalms she said, however, the sleepier she grew. After a while, her eyelids began to feel heavy as bricks.

And, in the end, though she fought to stay awake, her chin dropped, her eyes fastened shut. She fell asleep, sitting up, with her Bible on her lap.

Suddenly her eyes snapped open.

There was a crude scraping sound on the roof. She heard the zinc make a thumping noise. The unwanted visitor was here. It had returned, as promised; and this time, it would find a way in.

A small crack of light lay between the roof line and the outer wall of the house. A crack, no larger than a pencil. Yet it was an opening, an invitation for a prying hand or claw.

Flora ran toward the crack, tripping over the night table.

The candle flipped on its side, the hot wax burning her leg. She let out a little scream. Tearing off a piece of her nightgown, she leaped up, and stuffed it into the place where the crack let in the light.

Now the room was entirely black.

Flora retraced her steps, sat down on her mattress, and again waited. Outside a soft rain began to fall, pattering the banana leaves around the doorway.

"I'm safe," she told herself. "Whatever's out there can't get in. I'm perfectly safe."

However, no sooner had she said this, than the bit of cloth blew into the room, allowing a tiny seam of light to enter. The roof made a kind of shuddering sound, as something pried up the corrugated zinc. The force of foulness looked into the house. The crack in the roof grew larger. Something, unseen, slipped in.

Flora heard the sickening thud as the creature landed on the floor. It dropped with the meaty slackness of a reptile.

Flora knew what to do, for she'd rehearsed this part in her mind, as well as her body. Beside the mattress was a pail of water from the spring at the foot of Firefly Hill, the place where the mermaid lived. Flora had put sprigs of the leaf of life plant into the spring water.

Now, as she listened to the queer licking sound that filled the silence of the room, she picked up the pail of water and prepared to throw it on the intruder.

A zigzag of lightning cut across the sky. She saw it through the opening in the zinc—a scar of ragged light. She thought of the verse from Matthew, 24:27, that went, " . . . For as the lightning comes from the east and flashes to the west, so also will the coming of the Son of Man be."

"I pray the prophecy is true," Flora whispered, raising the pail of water.

There came another cut of light from the night sky, and in the sudden flare, Flora saw the thing that was coming after her.

It was the poison toad they called *bufo*. The creature whose flesh was so toxic that a mere brush with it could kill.

"Get away!" she cried.

The bufo moved with surprising dexterity. Flora heard its nails scratching on the tiles. She listened as it clawed a little closer. Now it was so close that she could smell the acrid odor of its breath.

The lightning came again, tearing the starless sky.

The bufo hopped to the edge of the mattress, yellow eyes agleam.

Flora had waited as long as she dared. Hefting the pail of water, she heaved it on the toad. The force of the blast struck the animal full in the face, throwing it backward.

Immediately, there rose up a sulfurous steam. The stench caused Flora's eyes to burn. Never in her life had she smelled anything so disgusting.

Again the lightning pulsated in the sky. And again Flora saw the bufo coming toward her.

Suddenly, limber as a cat, it hopped halfway across the floor.

For a moment she thought of stomping it—it was not much larger than her foot—but she was barefoot. The stomp might kill the animal, but it would also be fatal to Flora.

Leaning against the wall was a mop. Flora ran for it, grasped the handle, and whirling around, positioned herself for a strike.

The bufo stayed where it was, considering its options. Then, it trundled cautiously along, like a child with a limp.

Flora, whose back was to the wall, caught a glimpse of the bufo's glowing eyes. And, in that one unfortunate glance, the animal cast its spell onto her.

Flora stood helplessly, her face drawn with fear. Her feet felt like lead, she was rooted to the floor.

The bufo, sensing its advantage, took time coming to her.

Nearer. Slowly, nearer. Narrowing the distance between them.

As the bufo slimed along the floor, Flora began to work her lips. Softly, she began to sing the song of death that her ancestors had fashioned long ago to ward off evil beings.

The words came out of her mouth as if she had always known them, as if they were a part of her soft bones and watery blood. She felt her shadow power rising within. With her feet firmly planted, she felt a part of her float freely over the creature that was seeking to destroy her. Now she was the unseen shadow and the hideous bufo was the poison arrow nailed to the floor.

"*Mayombe, bombe, mayombe!*" she hissed.

The bufo heard the words, and stopped. It sat back on its haunches.

Flora repeated the song, louder than before.

"Mayombe, bombe, mayombe," she sang, "with sound I strike you, with words like clubs I strike you, mayombe, bombe, mayombe."

Her hands held the mop handle, but she was still incapable of moving it. Yet her voice, sibilant and soft, was very strong.

The ancient words had force, and the bufo feared them. Cautiously, it stuck out its deadly tongue, testing the air.

Flora drove the shadow chant into the bufo's face. And, looking fearlessly into its eyes, she saw a primordial swamp shrinking into a parched desert. She looked at its skin, the flesh of the desert cracking in the sun.

"Mayombe," Flora sang, "mayombe."

The bufo crawled forward. A trail, like that of a crushed snail, oozed behind it.

"I must kill it now," Flora thought, "but how?" Willing her shadow self into the shape of a sharp-beaked hen, she turned into a thing that dashed and dived, dipped and stabbed. With beak of fire and spurs of spark, she flew upon her foe in a dazzling feint of shadow feathers.

When Flora opened her eyes, morning had come. Roosters were crowing in the hibiscus bushes. She was leaning against the wall with a mop in her hand. The floor was wet, and there was a strange smell in the air as of something burning. She walked dumbly to the door and opened it.

The sunlight fell upon her, dazzling her eyes.

In the yard there was a white hen, gleaming in the tropical glow of the morning sun.

"Thanks and praises," Flora whispered. Then, "I vow, this day, never to eat chicken as long as I live!"

The old hen, eyeing the mop, scuttled out of Flora's way.

Some months later, Flora went to Zion Hill to visit

a friend, and heard that Chick Chick, the obeah man, had disappeared. On the morning of his disappearance, his neighbors found a white hen roosting on his pillow.

THE STORYTELLER SPEAKS

There were—and still are—sorcerers, obeah men, who live in the hills of St. Mary. Some people whom I knew wanted to meet one, and I took them there.

There were three of us present, four, counting the obeah man. Selecting a chair for himself, he presented us with three others, beckoning us to join him at a small table covered with a white lace tablecloth. The walls of the room were exactly as described in the story, full of ceramic icons.

Somehow, I felt a trick in the air. The table looked normal enough. The chairs, lacquered and sturdy, seemed in keeping with the place. I started to seat myself—but no, something told me to look under my chair.

I did—the chair had only three legs. Had I tried to

sit on it, I would've toppled to the floor. The clever obeah man had planned to unseat the curious teacher from Castle Gordon and make a fool of him.

However, observing the trick chair, I sat on it as if nothing were amiss. You can, if you balance yourself just right, sit on a three-legged chair. It was necessary to show the obeah man that I was not afraid of him.

"What is it that you have come to learn?" he asked after we had seated ourselves. Obeah men waste no time getting down to business.

I explained that one of us had a wife who was planning to leave the next day to return to the States. We wanted to know if he could guess which wife it was who was leaving.

The obeah man burst out laughing.

"Do you think you could possibly withhold such a thing from me?" he asked, his eyes sparkling.

No one else smiled.

"Very well," he said, "please take off your wedding ring and place it in this glass of water."

I did as requested, asking what kind of water was in the glass.

"Ordinary well water," he explained.

"Now I will read the names of the saints," he said, "and if your wife is leaving tomorrow, her guardian saint will know of it."

"What will happen then?"

"Your wedding ring will shake around in the glass."

Then he read a long list of saints, speaking the names so fast that none of us could understand a word he said. It sounded as if he were speaking in tongues. The ring lay quiet in the clear water of the glass.

The process was repeated with each of the others, with the effect that the last ring, belonging to the man whose wife was about to depart, began to move about in the glass, making a ringing sound.

All three of us were impressed. We then asked the obeah man to visit us the following day in Castle Gordon so that we might learn more of his magic. However, when our friends, the villagers, heard that this man was coming, they exercised some obeah of their own, and the obeah man never showed up. That was the last I ever saw of him. And the end of my obeah lessons.

As to the bufo legend related here, there are many such tales, similarly stated, around the islands. Bufo's common name is frog, though he is not a frog at all. There are seventeen species of frog on the island of Jamaica and only one toad. The bufo is clearly—and scientifically—a toad: Bufo marinus, the giant nocturnal marine variety. The poison glands of the bufo are

63

such that, though he may be handled safely, his skin should not, in any way be ingested. Voodoo ceremonies in Haiti combine the dried, ground flesh of the bufo with that of the puffer fish to make a toxin used in the practice of converting a person into what is commonly called a "zombie." The poison of the bufo slows the heartbeat, which may lead to heart failure. The powers of the bufo also stem naturally from its unusual—some would say ugly—amphibian appearance. The toad casting its "warts" on people, some say, comes from an ancient African legend.

The Jamaican proverb which calls the woman a shadow and the man an arrow serves Flora well in the mystical defense against the bufo. It is her shadow, not her physical presence, which defeats her enemy.

UNCLE
TIME

UNCLE TIME, THE SPIDERMAN, SPINS THE WEB
THAT COVERS THE WORLD WITH FATE.
~ *Proverb*

Uncle Time was a small, dark, West Indian man. No
one knew where he lived, or where he had come
from, but around him there grew a tangled wreath of
legends, a mist of truths, half-truths, and some out-
right lies. Rumor seemed to follow him wherever he
went. Someone said that he'd killed a man, done

some time in jail at Richmond Farm over by Highgate. But no one knew for sure.

One day Uncle Time appeared on the road between Castle Gordon and Port Maria. At the double bend in the road there was a Leyland truck, a huge diesel hauling gravel from the Wog Water stone pit.

And there was that small, dark, West Indian man, Uncle Time. He was walking along, seemingly unaware of the truck, but he was also directly in its path.

The big truck was bearing down.

The little man, in sight of the truck, made no move to get out of the way.

The horn blasted like a wounded bull.

The chrome grille of the diesel grinned murderously in the sun.

Seconds before collision, the little man leaped up and landed on the roof of the truck. He'd sailed twelve feet through the air, and alighted like a butterfly, unhurt. And it was as if it had never happened.

Legends like this spread all over Castle Gordon and into the hills of St. Mary. The townspeople dubbed him Uncle Time. They compared him to Anansi, the magic spiderman of Africa, the superhero whom no being—mortal or immortal—could kill.

One day a Chinese man named Chin was carrying a load of cane down Grant's Town hill. As it happened, he passed Uncle Time on the narrow goat trail by Blue Harbour. But when he turned to see if it was really Uncle Time, Chin saw only his own shadow. Where had the little man gone? He looked into a tree and saw Uncle Time reclining upon a limb, eating a Bombay mango.

Then there was the boy named Percy who had failed the Common Entrance Exam. He suffered such shame, this boy, that he planned to hang himself. And he went into the bush to do so. But once he got there, and had readied his noose for the big swing into eternity, who should he see but Uncle Time.

Uncle Time was watching the whole thing and smiling. He offered Percy some bananas from the bunch he'd just picked, and told him to stick around, and he might see something. They sat on the limb of a big *guango* tree, eating bananas and tossing the peels to the ground.

Presently, there appeared an old beggar man, so ragged and toothless that he couldn't care for himself any longer. The grimy beggar man, spying the pile of banana skins, fell upon them like a starving dog, and, growling, began to devour them. Percy—seeing someone far more unfortunate than himself—realized that his own situation was not so bad. He vowed never to try and take his own life again.

Once there was a fisherman named Milo. Milo used to go so far out to sea chasing tuna that he often fell asleep in his boat and woke up the next morning off the coast of Cuba. One time when he was on one of these distant sea journeys, he saw something that looked like a turtle, rising and settling in the tide.

He knew that it was very late in the day because when he left port, the sun was full on his chest. Now, heading home, the sun was still warming him there. Rising and setting, the sun was always by his heart, and that was how he knew where he was. Still, he was several miles out to sea when he saw this bobbing thing, rising and falling in the deep blue troughs.

Perhaps it is a turtle, he thought.

Then, he was close to it. What a surprise—the mysterious presence on the high seas was none other than Uncle Time, who explained that he was "just out for a swim."

Milo was amazed to see that Uncle Time, though he accepted a ride to shore, was not afraid of sharks nor even of drowning.

"You could die out here," Milo said, giving the small man his hand and pulling him in.

However, Uncle Time merely smiled and took a seat in the stern of the boat.

"Have you no fear?" Milo asked.

Uncle Time smiled and said nothing.

"A storm could come up and drown you!" Milo threatened.

Uncle Time said nothing.

For a while, it seemed that everyone in the town of Castle Gordon had a story about Uncle Time. Wherever he went, something extraordinary seemed to happen. He was, the people felt, a man of greatness. Yet many of the things he did were common and often passed unnoticed.

Now, as it happened, there came a night when some thieves were parceling out the spoils of a robbery. They'd taken refuge under the limbs of a wild fig tree, the roots of which went deep into the ground. It was a good place not to be seen. The three men were passing crumpled bills when a hundred dollar note dropped into one of the caves made by the roots of the wild fig.

"Lower yourself down dere, mon, and fetch me dat note," the leader said to one of his men.

"It too dark fe see," the man said, cringing in the shadows.

"Tek the flashlight down into de cave, mon, and carry the note up back."

Without further argument, the man slid down the fig root into the black cave.

"Fetch the note up back, mon," the leader shouted impatiently.

Now the man saw the note lying open before his eyes, but he also heard something in the cave that stopped him in his tracks.

"A ting growl down here," the man quavered.

He slid up the cabled root, just as the growls grew louder. All three men heard them by then.

"Run," the leader yelled, "it's a duppy."

The next morning the stolen money turned up on the doorstep of Miss June Chung, owner of Chung's Grocery in Port Maria. It was her store that had been robbed. All the money was returned, or most of it anyway.

"Me see him wid me own eye," one of the thieves, who was drinking at a rum shop, said later that night.

"What you see, mon? Stop your bawling and tell us—"

"Uncle Time."

After that, legends stretched out like a mystical web and covered the town. There was the tale of the burning mongoose . . . the beating heart in the paper bag . . . the rat-bat with the *bammy* cake in its mouth. . . .

And all of these tales were somehow imputed to Uncle Time. Whatever happened, for a while, was his doing. Be it normal or abnormal, Uncle Time was the unmoved mover, the thing around which all other things revolved. And yet, as the rumor mill ground out rumors, the people saw less and less of that little, dark, West Indian man.

Then word had it that Uncle Time was living in the ruins of an old Great House, a slave plantation, outside of Castle Gordon. The ruined house was surrounded by a ghostly garden of neglected flowers and trees. No one went there, for the place was crawling with duppies.

Now, as soon as it became known that Uncle Time was staying there, the three thieves decided to pay him a visit. They came one night well-armed with pistols and machetes.

"All right," the leader said, "You do what me se fe do, seen?"

The other two nodded, and answered, "Seen."

The plan seemed simple enough. They rounded the big breadfruit tree that sheltered the overgrown yard, and saw the little, dark man around whom so many legends and magic deeds had spun.

Uncle Time was squatting before a fire of pimento sticks, roasting a yam for his supper.

"Look pon him now," the leader scoffed, "him just a likkle mon." He spat on the ground, walked boldly into the firelight. The others, doglike, trailed behind.

The leader then strode up to Uncle Time, unholstered his revolver and emptied it into him.

The pistol shots shattered the still air, sending squeaking, flapping rat-bats up into the night sky.

Uncle Time was lying on the ground.

The leader cried out, "Him dead, me kill Uncle Time!"

First one thief, then the other stepped into the circle of firelight. What they saw made them feel queasy. The little man was lying on his side with his eyes tightly closed. They couldn't have explained why, but the sight made them ill.

"Chop him!" the leader commanded.

The two men made no movement.

"Chop him!" he screamed.

Then something strange happened.

From out of the quivering trees came cords of silk. The thieves felt them bind their heads and shoulders, their arms and ankles, and though they struggled to get free, their bodies were soon sealed with silken bonds as strong as steel.

The thieves were bound from head to foot; the silk fell from the sky, and turned them into cocoons of snow.

Mummified, they remained. Frozen in place.

This is how the townspeople of Castle Gordon found the three thieves the following morning. And if you ask someone in Castle Gordon what happened to those men, he or she will point to the nearest tree and show you the magic web of Anansi, breathing sweetly in the sunlight, bowing in the wind.

So that is all there is to say of the three thieves.

Of Uncle Time, however, more can always be said.

You may see him on sunny days and gloomy days, sitting under his favorite palm tree over by Pagee Beach, or up on the peninsula, by Black Sand. He has nowhere to go, and nothing to do. But he is always around, and people are always talking about him, saying this, that, and the other.

Somehow, you can usually find people gathered around, making idle remarks about how he lives, and what life would be like without him. But, no matter what they say about him, the people know, now and forever more, that you can't kill Uncle Time.

Nor can you make a fool out of Anansi.

THE STORYTELLER SPEAKS

There is a school teacher, Mrs. Soley, who runs a primary school in Grant's Town, just above the village of Castle Gordon. Some days, when she is feeling a touch of "the pressure," which makes the head dizzy and the feet numb, she sits down under her coffee tree and tells the children all about her two friends, Truth and Justice.

Now to hear Mrs. Soley speak, you would never know that these two outstanding citizens of St. Mary were, essentially, words. You would never guess that they were symbols. Listening to Mrs. Soley, you would swear that Truth and Justice were a couple of friends, who lived in Grant's Town.

And so it is in Jamaica.

Uncle Time, though, came not from the enterprising sermons of Mrs. Soley, but from a tale told by Benji Oswald Brown, a groundskeeper of Blue Harbour, Castle Gordon.

Benji's Uncle Time was actually a man called

Cheeto. He got this name, Benji said, by way of cheating Mr. Death so many times. An Anansi character, Cheeto traveled the hills, just like Uncle Time, not doing much of anything. Yet wherever he went, he made friends and, of course, enemies. He was—by his very nature—the blessing that time allows. Much good came of meeting him.

How many times Mr. Death tried to capture him, no one knew. However, there were countless tales, a few of which have been mentioned here. The name Uncle Time came to me from a poem of Jamaican poet, Dennis Scott. In one of his verses, he says:

Uncle Time is a spider-man, cunning an' cool,
. . . 'im move like mongoose; man, yu t'ink 'im fool?

According to Benji, Cheeto, Uncle Time's blood and bone counterpart, is an incarnation of that old African spider trickster, Anansi. Benji says Cheeto has a peculiar smile, which can turn dark as sorrow or light as joy. His voice is soft as the bamboo leaf bowing in the breeze. His humor is dry as donkey tobacco and, often, just as bitter. He seems to be all things to all people. And only those who have been deprived of him know the loss.

DUPPY TALK

ONLY WHEN YOU HAVE CROSSED THE RIVER CAN YOU SAY WHETHER IT WAS A CROCODILE OR A FLOATING STICK THAT YOU SAW THERE.

~ *Proverb*

"Tell me the one about the shadow catcher," the boy, Usie, begged.

"I told you that one yesterday," the storyteller said.

"But I want to hear it again."

"Don't you ever get enough of that story?"

Usie shook his head solemnly.

"I could listen to that story all the time."

Jacob, the storyteller, was a student of folklore at the University of the West Indies. His specialty was ghost stories, duppy tales. Most of what he knew he'd learned in school, but now he was traveling around the island, harvesting stories from old storytellers. When he wasn't collecting, he was storytelling himself. Which was how he'd met Usie whose hunger for hauntings was beyond measure.

"Let's see," Jacob said, "you want to hear more about shadow catching?"

Usie nodded as he tore apart a piece of sugar cane with his teeth. His eyes were on Jacob, just as his teeth were on the cane.

"You won't have teeth much longer, if you keep that up," Jacob remarked.

But Usie, absorbed in his feast, went on with his ritual chewing.

A sea breeze played at their feet. In the distance, well beyond the reef, the sun was sinking. The hills were turning tangerine in the light. Soon they would be gray. After which evening would come upon them, by degrees. The tops of the pimento trees would be the last to darken. Then the nightingale would stop singing and Patoo, the owl, would start to call from deep within the bush.

Slowly, as if unraveling threads, Jacob began to tell what he knew of shadow catching, the ancient art of sorcery.

"In the old days," he began, "the obeah man kept a little coffin around his neck. He used this to capture the wandering souls, that went about at night."

"What souls?" Usie asked.

"Any souls that happened to be around. You know, when a shadow—that is, a spirit—leaves your body when you sleep, sometimes it gets lost in the dream world."

"Is that what happens when people go crazy?"

"Sometimes, yes. Back in the old days, when this happened, people called on the shadow catcher to get the lost soul back into its body. The shadow catcher would find the lost soul and put it into a little coffin that he wore around his neck. Then he would hang that coffin on the trunk of a silk-cotton tree."

Usie spat out some of the sugar cane. "A great big soul in that teeny little coffin?"

Jacob chuckled. "Who has ever measured the size of a soul?"

Usie allowed that he hadn't, and went on eating his cane.

"So how would the shadow catcher set the shadows free?"

Jacob gazed down into the pasture of the old plantation where they were sitting. He could see an enormous silk-cotton tree whose limbs were spread more than 150 feet across the pasture. He imagined the slave women gathered round in their white, cassava-starched dresses, their turbaned heads wrapped in white. He could see them now—in his mind's eye—pelting the silk-cotton tree with hen's eggs, as was the ancient custom. He could imagine the shadow catcher carrying a bowl of fresh spring water and placing it under the mighty ancestor tree.

"Now," Jacob said, trying to shake the vision, "the obeah man would open the little coffin and let the shadow out. Then the lost soul would enter a bowl of water."

"What good is a bowl of water?" Usie frowned, wiping cane juice from his lips.

"Well," Jacob reasoned, "the water is the proper medium in which to trap a soul."

"Where was the person who'd lost his soul in the first place?"

"Sitting around somewhere—like this—"

Jacob made a blank face.

"So," Jacob continued, "The spellbound soul is

then given back to its owner. The shadow catcher just pours the water over the head of the soulless person, and he or she is normal again."

"Cool!" Usie cried. "Hey, Jacob, what's the wickedest story you ever heard?"

Jacob ran his fingers through his hair.

"I suppose," he replied, "that would have to be the tale of the yellow boa. People used to say there were snakes that would 'set for them.' That meant they'd hide in the trees, drop down on people's necks, and strangle them."

Usie looked at the pimento tree where Jacob had strung his hammock.

"Don't worry, yellow boas don't like pimento trees."

"Why not?"

"Maybe they don't like pimentos."

"Do you know any more about the snakes?" Usie asked.

"After the yellow boa strangles you, they say that he sucks the blood out of you."

"Can a snake really do that?"

"Only a mythological snake. According to legend, it draws the blood out through the nose. Takes a whole night to drain a man dry."

"Wicked!"

"Yes, it's wicked, all right."

"You know any more about snakes?"

"Well, I heard a story over in Sav-La-Mar. An old granny told me about a couple of yellow snakes, husband and wife, she called them. They moved around at night, upright, she said, on the ends of their tails."

"For real?" Usie said.

"That's what they say, anyway."

"And that's the worst you ever heard?"

"No," Jacob admitted, "the worst I ever heard was when a woman over in St. Elizabeth gave birth to a yellow snake."

"You got to be kidding," Usie cried.

Jacob continued, "The poor woman brought forth not one, but several yellow snakes."

Usie threw his cane stalk into the shadows of the coming night. "Never, never heard nothing like that!" he said in disgust. "Well, I gotta be going home now. See you in the morning, Jacob."

"Hey, Usie. Tell your mother how much I liked her sweet potato pie."

"I'll tell her," Usie shouted as he ran off through the pasture. Jacob watched Usie's white T-shirt bob across the violet dusk and disappear in the tall guinea grass at the edge of the pasture. Jacob didn't know why he liked telling stories to Usie so much, but perhaps it was the way the boy gave himself over to them. He acted as if every word that Jacob said was gospel. Even when doubtful, Usie was still an old believer.

Jacob lay back in the hammock he'd set up. Where else, he wondered, could a man lie outdoors on a summer night and be unmolested by a fly, flea, mosquito—or even a passerby.

Yawning, Jacob wondered if he would ever write the stories that he enjoyed telling to children. One day, he thought, one day. Then he tugged the nylon poncho over himself, in case it rained, closed his eyes, and went straight to sleep.

Jacob woke with a start when he felt something resting on his foot. He came out of sleep like a swimmer who was well below the surface and who suddenly comes up for air.

Instantly awake, he regarded his right foot which felt heavy. In the half-light, he saw the snake coiled around his big toe, the heavy, triangular head poised at eye level, ready to strike.

At once a wave of nausea filled his stomach and rose toward his throat. He fought it back, trying to remain calm. Then he broke into a cold sweat.

Glancing at his foot without moving, he saw that the snake had slid through the hammock webbing and cradled its upper body on his bare foot.

The pointed head was weaving ever so slightly. Jacob imagined the forked tongue flipping in and out of its closed mouth. The smooth belly scales lay long and limber on his foot. He cursed himself for going to sleep with bare feet.

What can I do? he wondered.

A flick of the foot, a karate kick. No, that would result in a bite. The snake was already positioned to bite him. The shape of the head indicated that it was a venomous reptile, a *fer-de-lance*. Jacob knew that a bite from one of these snakes sent the body into immediate convulsions.

Now what?

He sought some access to safety. If he were quick enough, he could reverse the hammock—flip it like a flapjack. This would knock the snake to the ground. But it would also dump him on top of it.

Then it came to him—the stick he used for hiking was next to his head. Inches away, he could seize it and strike the snake in the head.

Jacob had learned stick throwing in the hills of St.

Mary. He was an expert. He could execute a thrust that would send the snake into the next parish.

He lay perfectly still, planning the steps he must take. First, take hold of the stick which was resting against the hammock. Second, strike with the accuracy of a mongoose.

He knew that he could not afford to miss—or to hesitate for even a second. The whole tactic rested upon his ability to strike. Fortunately, it was his forte. He'd once nailed a dragonfly to a stump at one hundred paces.

Now, while monitoring his breathing, he studied the head of the snake. Inert but attentive, the thick head was a dark diamond-shaped target against the moon-filled meadow.

Very well then, he thought. Now or never.

Now—

Like lightning, he seized the stick, and quick as an arrow released from a drawn bow, he flung it at the snake's head, snapped his foot back under him and flipped the hammock. The last image his mind retained before he hit the ground was the snake flying end over end into the grass.

He was on his feet in a heartbeat, pounding the creature into the ground. Adrenalin poured through his body as he pulverized the deadly snake.

Then, with extreme repulsion, he stuck the stick into the lifeless coils and lifted it up. But before he could examine it more closely, he heard a weird squeal in the bush. Looking up, Jacob saw something dart into the shadows. It didn't look like a wild pig, but that was what it sounded like.

The squeal sounded again, farther off. A wild boar drawn to the blood feast of a fer-de-lance, Jacob thought.

Then, for the first time, he looked carefully at the thing he'd just killed, the object of his worst nightmare. The snake, Jacob now realized, was an old piece of hemp. He flung it on the ground.

Somewhere, in the sanctuary of the tall grass, piglike squeals echoed through the bush. These, too, Jacob now recognized.

THE STORYTELLER SPEAKS

This story came from my father, who traveled in the Caribbean in the 1930s. As a child I heard the tale many times; as an adult I have told it myself at many a storytelling gathering.

Jacob is a portrait of the author as a young story-teller—learning his trade, the hard way.

Usie is a trickster who lives outside of Castle Gordon, in Oracabessa. He loves to play tricks on people who think they know more than they do.

As a storyteller I learned a valuable lesson in Jamaica: Let the legend shape you, before you try to shape the legend. In other words, you must know the tale personally, culturally, and emotionally before it can become yours in the retelling. Stories are meant to be shared. Myths are part of the consciousness of humankind. However, as they say, seeing is better than hearing; a storyteller must immerse himself/herself in the truth of the experience. This means, of course, really living it.

And, then again, how can you see what is not there?

Duppies, I learned, come to those who wait. While those who jump to conclusions, like Jacob in the story, are bitten, so to speak, by their own haste.

Duppies, unlike hemp snakes, seem to exist; I believe they do, anyway.

But like all things beyond the realm of our senses, they must be felt to be understood. The heart must leap before the mind can follow where the heart has gone.

Then, and only then, can the traveler speak of what he saw in the dark water of the river at night, or in the flame tree at dusk, or in the blue spring during the glare of noon.

The things that we like—and don't like—to imagine are merely waiting to enchant us. So, unfortunately, are the world's illusions. Which is why, only when you have crossed the river, can you say whether it was a crocodile or a floating stick that you saw there.

THE PROVERBS OF DUPPY TALK

African wisdom declares that proverbs are the horses of conversation. When talk among people grows tired, a fresh proverb may be mounted and ridden; and thus, the talk is carried a bit further up the road.

The proverbs in this book originally came from Africa. Yet they have become, over the years, a reflection of Jamaica and the Jamaican people. These folk sayings embody a natural affection for wisdom and words used for the sake of utility, as well as philosophy. It is said that fools argue and don't get anywhere but that wise men recite proverbs and thus solve problems.

The proverb *Seeing is different from being told* is the same as saying—to use another Jamaican expression—*Who feels it knows it.* Proverbs are like distilled water. Hundreds of years of sifting through the rock beds of human trial and error have produced the clear water of wisdom. However, we know nothing, unless we have seen it with our own eyes, or walked on it with our own feet. So the proverb *Seeing is different from being told* is actually a proverb about the nature of proverbs. We must *see* in order to *know*; otherwise we are hearing empty words.

The human eye offers but one way of seeing. A far more important "eye" is in the heart and in the mind. *The mind doesn't see what the heart can't leap* means that only when the heart speaks can the mind truly *know* something. Again, this is quite like the expression *To feel it is to know it,* for it emphasizes the heart, which has a "mind" of its own.

The proverb *When one door is closed, another is opened* is identified with reggae prophet Bob Marley because he used it in his song, "Coming in from the Cold." However, much of his writing came from Jamaican folk sayings. Besides stating a physical law—that matter moves along, flowing from one source to another—it also makes clear the spiritual truth: that when something is lost, something else is found.

The woman is like a shadow; the man is like an arrow refers, in Jamaican usage, to the directness of the male approach to life and the indirectness of the female. This is not meant to be chauvinistic, or to place men and women apart. It merely shows that their power of expression is quite different. The mystic power of the shadow can escape the warrior power of the arrow. The arrow, in fact, cannot overcome the secrecy of the shadow. So, the arrow may be a metaphor of man, and of daylight; and the shadow may be a metaphor of woman, and of night.

Uncle Time, the spiderman, spins the web that covers the world with fate says that life, wrapped in fate, is a mysterious thing. For instance, when time and chance are on our side, giving us what we want, they are just like Anansi, who saves the day and makes everyone smile. However, when our luck is down and getting worse, then it is as if Anansi were conspiring against us. So it is that life brings both joy and grief, and if you know one, you shall, in the course of time, which is the net of Anansi, come to know the other.

When you have crossed the river, you should know what the river is like, and how it feels to cross over it. The ancient Ashanti proverb *Only when you have crossed the river can you say whether it was a crocodile or a floating stick that you saw there* once again refers to the importance of experience when making wise judgments about life. The river, then, is a picture of life itself. Wide and many-folded, full of fast currents and tricky turns, the river is most difficult to cross. To know the river's moods, a man or woman must travel upon it. And, in so doing, he/she learns what dangers—crocodiles—lurk below the surface; and how such dangers are met, not with words alone, but with deeds of daring.

All of these Afro-Jamaican proverbs seem to say that there is no substitute for experience. Yes, this is certainly true. However, since proverbs come from experience, when we say them, do we not—in some way—live in their special truth? As the saying goes, *To listen is to learn; one must talk little, and listen much.*

GLOSSARY

Anansi   The spider-trickster of Afro-Jamaican lore is a comical and witty fellow whose mystical powers are combined with common sense and a fun-loving nature.

Arawak Indians   The first inhabitants of the island of Jamaica, these Amerindian people are thought to have migrated from South America. They were present on many of the Caribbean islands when Columbus arrived from Europe.

Ashanti   A West African tribe brought to Jamaica during the colonial or slave era. There are many people of Ashanti origin on the north coast of Jamaica.

bammy   A kind of fried bread, usually eaten with fish, and made from the cassava root.

breadfruit   Introduced to Jamaica in 1792 from Tahiti, this is a broad-fingered leaf tree that bears a green fruit that is a staple in the island diet. It is commonly served roasted.

bufo   This large marine toad, because of its poison glands, is sometimes used by sorcerers. If ingested, the powder made from bufo flesh and crushed puffer fish can render a person comatose. A large enough dose of the poison will induce heart failure.

bush doctor   One who uses natural herbs and plant medicines to cure physical and mental illness.

cassava   A popular root of the West Indies and Central and South America. The Arawaks baked cassava bread which was considered a holy or sacred food. Jamaicans use cassava as a starch for eating, as well as for laundry.

cerasee   A well-known tea leaf in Jamaica, cerasee comes from a wild vine that grows everywhere. People say that cerasee can cure almost anything, but it is a very bitter drink. Rural Jamaicans drink the tea as a purifier of the blood.

chick–chick Jamaican thrushes have a surprising number of names, of which this is one. There is also the "tricking chick" or "chickin' chick," who digs up the farmer's fresh-planted corn. The "chick-mon-chick" is an ash-colored, red-beaked thrush whose three-note song resembles its name. When you hear this bird sing in the early morning, before first light, it may mean that someone is going to die. In the story "Chick Chick," the obeah man shares a little of all of these suggestive names.

cocoa bread A delicious risen bread often served with melted butter. A particular favorite for lunch.

Common Entrance Exam The rigorous test taken by primary school students in order to determine eligibility into high school.

creeper vine Widely known in the Jamaican back country as a *withe* or *wiss,* this jungle vine hangs from trees and appears to creep—hence the name.

duppy   Jamaican ghost, or spirit of the dead, based on the African idea that there are two spirits or souls; after death one remains on earth and lingers a while, or even permanently, while the other goes on to heaven, or the spirit world. The spirit that lingers on earth is usually associated with evil or wrongdoing, but it may also be misled, or abused, by an obeah man, or sorcerer. Duppies can also be playful and prankish and relatively harmless. The word duppy is believed to come from the African *dupe*, or ghost. However, there is another unlikely yet amusing explanation: It is said that duppy is a corruption of doorpeep, one who peers through a keyhole.

fish tea   Actually a fish soup, this "tea" is made of vegetables and fresh fish and makes a complete meal in one serving.

flame of the forest   Also known as the *African tulip tree* or *flame heart,* this tree has huge orange blossoms, a very large trunk, and spreading branches.

gourdy Also called *goady,* this is a calabash tree native to Central and South America and the West Indies. From the time of the Arawak Indians up to the present, the gourd produced by this tree has been used as a multipurpose container, canteen, soup bowl, etcetera. It can also be made into a musical instrument. Once dried, the gourd is filled with pebbles and used as a kind of maraca. The pulp of the gourd, mixed with kerosene oil, is used to extract poison from wounds.

Great House Common Jamaican name for a plantation house built during the Colonial era.

guango Native to South America, the guango is one of the largest trees on the island of Jamaica. It is often regarded with suspicion because the grass under the tree is usually greener than the pasture grass that grows around it.

irie Jamaican patois word associated with the Rastafarian religion. It means well being, joy to all, happiness.

John Crow Also *Johncrow, turkey vulture,* or *carrion crow*; the name stems from an unpopular preacher in Jamaica. The bird's black plumage and bold red head reminded people of the Reverend John Crow, an Irish clergyman serving time in Jamaica. The story is told of how he preached a sermon in which he asked other prisoners, who had been transported to Jamaica with him, to submit without complaint to their unjust masters.

kananga water An alcohol-based, perfumed toilet water. It is frequently used in Jamaica to sponge bathe someone who is feverish.

kaya mattress This is made from the dry, brown husk of the coconut. The fiber is separated from the shell-like outer husk and used as mattress stuffing.

leaf of life Succulent plant used in folk medicine or bush cures. Even a piece of it, if planted, will grow new leaflets.

macka tree *Macka* or *macca* in Jamaican patois means "a thorn or something sharp that will stick you." A macka tree, then, is a thorn tree. The name is a corruption of the Spanish *macaw*; long ago, these colorful birds were often seen in various thorn trees on the island.

mermaid Also called *river mother*, or, in patois: *rivah moomah*, which may be translated as *river mommy*. The Jamaican version of the legend goes back to the Arawak chief whose golden treasure was guarded by a mermaid. When a Spanish explorer once tried to steal the mermaid's golden comb, she drowned him.

myal Mystical practice of communing with spirits, using bush lore and bush medicine. Myalism is also known as white magic.

nine night Similar to an Irish wake, nine night is based on the idea that a dead person's spirit should have a nice send-off from this world. If done properly, nine night insures that the duppy will not return to haunt the living.

obeah Also called *science* by Jamaicans, obeah is a kind of black magic or sorcery brought from West Africa to the islands of the Caribbean.

patois The informal and colloquial language of the West Indies. Patois, which is comprised of various languages—English, French, Spanish, African, to name a few—is a lively and living, fully adaptive language, that changes constantly as words and phrases are added and subtracted according to the times. Jamaican patois still uses old forms of African speech, the syntax of the slaves who had come from various parts of Africa. Since the slaves were many tribes and many nations, they had to develop a language that would fit the needs of all. Patois is that language—alive and well 400 years later.

patoo Also spelled *patu*, this is the patois word in Jamaica for owl. The same word is used in West Africa, particularly Ghana. In Arawak stories, patoo is the bringer of darkness in the world of legends.

penner   A farmer or man who tends cattle and usually carries a long whip.

pickney   Also spelled *pickni* or *pickny,* the word may be a condensation from *pickaninny*; but it may also come from the Spanish *pequeno*. In any case, a pickney is a child, or when loosely used, the term means a young one and can refer to animals as well as children.

pimento   The handsome tree of the myrtle family produces a berry which is processed and used worldwide as allspice. The wood, when burned, makes a fragrant charcoal that is used in making Jamaica's famous jerk chicken.

poinciana   A beautiful tropical tree with red-orange blossoms. It is also known as *flamboyant*, or *flamboyant tree.*

rat-bat   A variety of tropical bat commonly seen in Jamaica, hanging upside down. For this reason, there is a legend which states that the bat, by pointing its rear end at heaven, is very disrespectful.

rolling calf A spirit or duppy that rolls and roars and falls downhill, clanking chains. This is a restless spirit, often associated with tales of slavery and dishonesty; it might, therefore, represent a tyrannical person, perhaps the wicked owner of a large estate.

roti East Indian flat bread, similar to a Mexican tortilla.

shadow catchers Either obeah men or myalists seeking to capture a duppy, or, as in the slave times, drawing it out of an ancestor tree known as the *silk-cotton*.

silk-cotton tree Probably the largest tree in Jamaica (growing up to 130 feet high), this native of tropical America was used by the Arawaks to make seagoing canoes. Afro-Jamaican stories tell of the spirits of ancient ancestors that reside within the wood. Thus, it has been called a *duppy tree*.

sulkies The half-man, half-seal sulky is of Celtic origin. The creature came to Jamaica through the stories of Irish mariners and landowners. However, there are also African legends that are similar.

witch doctor Generally, this term is used to cover white and black magic: myal and obeah. However, exaggerated use of the expression has given it a negative association. Bush doctors and other plant-healers and herbalists have also been labeled witch doctors, and it is now frequently associated with voodoo in a negative way.

yellow snake A very rare member of the boa constrictor family, which was once widely dispersed throughout the island of Jamaica. The African name for yellow snake is *nanka*. Today it is nearly extinct, due to the African folk belief which insists that the snake is dangerous to humans.